W9-AQZ-686

GUYS' GUIDES

Stay Cool

A Guy's Guide to Handling Conflict

Chris Hayhurst

the rosen publishing group's
rosen central
new york

Published in 2000 by The Rosen Publishing Group, Inc.
29 East 21st Street, New York, NY 10010

Copyright © 2000 by The Rosen Publishing Group, Inc.

First Edition

Library of Congress Cataloging-in-Publication Data

Hayhurst, Chris.
    Stay cool : a guy's guide to handling conflict/ Chris Hayhurst.—1st ed.
      p. cm. —(Guys' guides)
    Includes bibliographical references and index.
    Summary: Examines various types of conflicts and suggests ways of solving them satisfactorily and peacefully.
      ISBN 0-8239-3159-5
      1.Conflict management—Juvenile literature. 2. Teenage boys—Psychology—Juvenile literature. 3. Teenage boys—Conduct of life—Juvenile literature. 4. Young men—Psychology—Juvenile literature. 5. Young men—Conduct of life—Juvenile literature. [1. Conflict management.] I. Title. II. Series.

HM1126.H382000
303.6'921—dc21
                                                    99-041433

Manufactured in the United States of America

17.95

<<< Contents >>>

>> About this book <<

It's not easy being a guy these days. You're expected to be buff, studly, and masculine, but at the same time, you're supposed to be sensitive, thoughtful, and un-macho. And that's not all. You have to juggle all of this while you're wading through the shark-infested waters of middle school. So not only are you dealing with raging hormones, cliques and geeks, and body changes, but you're also supposed to figure out how to be a Good Guy. As if anyone is even sure what that means anyway. It's enough to make you wish for the caveman days, when guys just grunted and wrestled mammoths with their bare hands and stuff.

Being an adolescent is complicated. Take girls, for example. Just five minutes ago—or so it seems—they weren't much different from you and your buddies. Now, suddenly you can't keep your eyes off them, and other parts of your body have taken an interest too. Or maybe you're not interested in girls yet, and you're worried about when you will be. Then there's figuring out where you fit into the middle school world. Are you a jock, a brain, or what? And how come it seems that someone else gets to decide for you? What's up with that?

Yeah, it's tough. Still, you're a smart guy, and you'll figure it all out. That's not to say that we can't all use a hand. That's where this book comes in. It's sort of a cheat sheet for all the big tests that your middle school years throw at you. Use it to help you get through the amazing maze of your life—and to come out alive on the other side.

There's no doubt about it—being a guy isn't always easy. In fact, the ins and outs of everyday living, from what to wear to school to making friends to just plain growing up, can be downright challenging. The truth is, there's a lot to think about when you're a guy and a lot to go through before you become a man.

One of the biggest challenges on the rugged road to adulthood is how to deal with conflict. Unfortunately conflict—whether it's an argument between two people

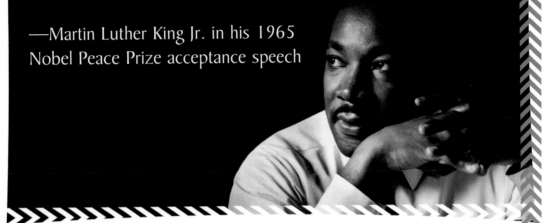

Cool Quote

"Sooner or later, all the people of the world will have to discover a way to live together in peace. . . . If this is to be achieved, man must evolve for all human conflict a method which rejects revenge, aggression, and retaliation. The foundation of such a method is love."

—Martin Luther King Jr. in his 1965 Nobel Peace Prize acceptance speech

or a war between two nations—is a fact of life. Everybody is different, so everyone has different ideas of what is right and what is wrong. People want different things, and sometimes those desires conflict with one another. When you put people together in one place, those differences are bound to cause difficulties. Take school, for instance: Have you ever seen a fight break out?

Conflict isn't always a bad thing. If you take it for what it is—a sign of individuality; of the small differences in every person on the planet that make life, relationships, and the world in general so interesting—you can use conflict to become a better man. You see, if you can face this challenge, the challenge of confronting conflict head-on, with your brain turned on and your fists turned down, you'll find that being a guy is a little less difficult. If you stay cool when you're faced with a conflict, you might even find that the road to adulthood—to becoming a man—isn't so bumpy after all.

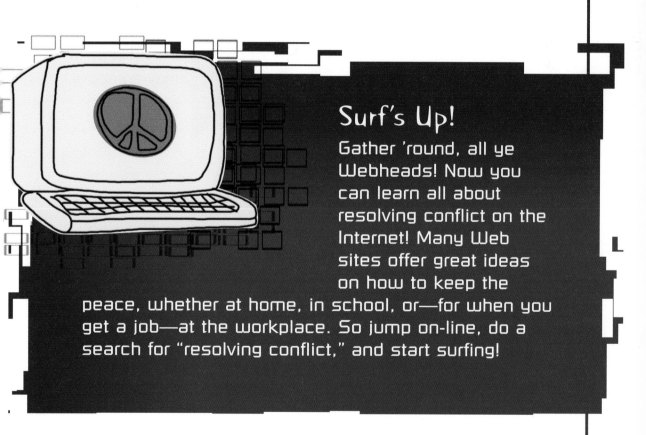

Surf's Up!

Gather 'round, all ye Webheads! Now you can learn all about resolving conflict on the Internet! Many Web sites offer great ideas on how to keep the peace, whether at home, in school, or—for when you get a job—at the workplace. So jump on-line, do a search for "resolving conflict," and start surfing!

2 <<< Conflict: A Fact of Life >>>

How you choose to deal with individual conflicts will play an important part in defining who you are and how you will be perceived as an adult. Will you consider the countless differences between yourself and every other person on the planet as a gift, or will you use diversity as an excuse to fight? If you choose to fight, you'll find that the good things in the world—like friendships, for instance—become more difficult to attain. If you choose to be tolerant and work out differences in a peaceful, understanding manner, these differences can contribute to a lifetime of happiness.

The answer, then, is easy: Avoid violence and practice peace.

The act of avoiding violence is not always easy, however. The reality is that conflict is everywhere, and where there's conflict, there's often the potential for violence. As long as differences exist between people—and they always will—there will be conflict. People hold many different points of view, opinions, ideas, and beliefs. There are people of various ethnicities, nationalities, and religions. Some people are poor, others are rich. Every person on earth is unique. Everyone carries a one-of-a-kind set of characteristics everywhere he goes.

If you think about it, conflict is only natural. People bump into each other with their bodies and their minds. What can you expect with so many different personalities roaming the world, meeting each other, and interacting with one another?

OK. Once you've accepted that conflict is a fact of life, you're ready to move on. You're ready for a resolution!

> Talkin' 'Bout a Resolution <

Even the worst conflicts can be resolved peacefully. But to understand how, it's best to take a look at some of the conflicts we go through every day, sometimes without even realizing it. When you see that conflicts are normal day in and day out, you'll begin to understand how resolutions, or answers, can be found for just about all of them.

Here's an example: You think that chocolate is the best ice cream flavor, whereas your friend prefers vanilla. You're at the ice cream shop together and have enough money between the two of you to buy only one pint. You can't buy both flavors. Which one do you choose?

Do you size each other up and start throwing punches? Of course not. Obviously, you and your friend are not going to get into a fistfight over which flavor to buy. Somehow you'll find a resolution that makes you both happy. Perhaps you'll buy a pint of strawberry instead—a flavor you both like. Maybe you'll take a second look at the menu and decide to get two small cones, one chocolate and one vanilla, for the same amount of money you'd spend on a pint. The point is, you'll negotiate; you'll come to an agreement. Rather than insisting that all of your needs be met, you'll move to middle ground, where satisfaction is guaranteed for all. In the end, you and your friend will both be happy, and you'll both get to eat ice cream. Case closed.

But wait. Not so fast. You can learn a lot from something as simple and delicious as ice cream. The key is to remember that each individual enters into a conflict with a list of his favorite flavors in mind. If you're on one end of that argument and you know what your intentions are—chocolate, vanilla, or whatever—be prepared to listen to the other side's intentions and to talk about your own feelings and opinions. It's a simple matter: If you're going to resolve a conflict peacefully, you have to be willing to use your tongue. Talk it out!

Licking Violence Together

Speaking of ice cream, how about a double scoop for Ben and Jerry's? In addition to its standard routine of stuffing pint containers full of delicious ice cream, this world-famous company has worked with the Massachusetts-based Educators for Social Responsibility (ESR) and their Resolving Conflict Creatively program to bring peace to schools across America. For more information on this program, contact ESR at 23 Garden Street, Cambridge, Massachusetts 02138; (617) 492-1764. Or visit their Web site at *www.esrnational.org*.

Conflict: A Reality at Every Level

Conflicts can occur in all aspects of life. Sometimes a conflict can be as minor as a question in one's own mind; at other times a conflict has the potential to be as large as a worldwide war. The list below explains the different kinds of conflict you might come across during your lifetime.

> Intrapersonal: An internal conflict whose resolution will primarily affect your. For example, will you do drugs, or will you choose to be drug-free?

> Interpersonal: A conflict between two people. For example, you get in an argument with a classmate over where you will sit during lunch.

> Intergroup: A conflict between two groups. For example, an opponent trips a player on your soccer team, and both teams argue over whether a foul was committed.

> Societal: A conflict in society. For example, conflicts due to skin color (racism) or gender (sexism).

> International: A conflict between two or more nations. For example, war.

International

Societal

Intrapersonal

Interpersonal

<<< Everyone Is Different >>>

3

One of the keys to learning how to resolve conflict peacefully is understanding diversity. You have to be able to accept other people and the lifestyles, thoughts, and opinions that they hold. You also have to accept that no one else in this world is exactly like you. Since you're unique, some of your characteristics are bound to conflict with those of other people, just as their characteristics are bound to conflict with yours. Keep these things in mind, and you'll be well on your way to keeping the peace.

Take a look around you. Maybe you're in the library or in a classroom. Maybe you're outdoors, in a park or square. Study the people near you. On the outside, you can see physical differences between them and yourself quite easily. Gender, body size, skin color, hairstyle, choice of clothing—these all stand out. There may also be ethnic, cultural, and national differences.

Inside, things get a little more complex. Each person is his own machine. Every individual has his own collection of feelings and emotions, his own memories of past experiences, and his own personal hopes for

the future. Some people seem to always be happy—as if nothing could get them down. Others never seem to stop frowning. Some kids seem as if they're angry at the world, whereas others are friends with everyone. Adults too share similar characteristics.

Now take a good hard look at yourself. Who are you, really? What type of person do you want to become? Can you think of times in your past that have shaped the way you are now?

OK. Here's the hard part: How do you fit in with other people? Take a look at your closest friends. Think about the people that you would never talk to in a million years. Why do you feel that way? Consider those who

make you angry or uneasy when you see them, those who rub you the wrong way for one reason or another. Do some people make you tense, whereas others make you feel relaxed?

Chances are, your observations—what you see—and your answers to all of these questions are hard to put into words. The truth is, we often have no idea who we are and who we want to be, now and as an adult. We're not quite sure why we don't accept some people into our groups of friends or why certain people don't show any interest in becoming our friends. In many cases, there's really no reason why we don't talk to one person or the other, or why that same person doesn't talk to us.

Often when we see differences between ourselves and other people, we avoid those people. We distance ourselves from those who aren't like us. We prefer to hang around our pals—people who share our interests, like the same sports, the same books, or the same games. There's no problem with wanting to hang out with your buddies. That's one of the best things about being a guy. But it helps to understand that those differences you see in people outside your circle of friends represent fantastic opportunities for you to grow as a man.

Think about what you can learn from someone who is different from you—someone from another country, for instance. Maybe he speaks only a few words of English. Maybe he speaks English but is afraid to use it because he thinks that you and your friends might poke fun at him for making mistakes. If you accept that person for who he is and respect the challenge he is faced with in immersing himself in a new culture, you stand to learn a thing or two about him and about the world.

The world today is a very small place filled with all types of people. Everyone depends on everyone else to live and to make a living. Countries depend on one another for food, protection, money, and millions of other things. Faraway cities are connected by phone lines, airlines, and the Internet. Television and radio bring news from distant countries into our living rooms. Student exchange programs bring kids from all over the globe into our classrooms. You rely on your teammates to help you win games. You depend on your teachers and classmates to help you learn about science, math, and English. You rely on

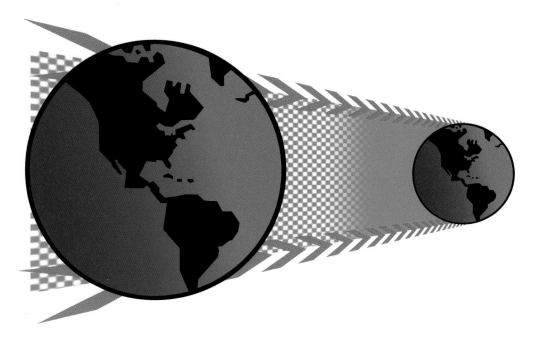

your parents to feed you and to give you a place to live. Every one of these people on whom you depend on day in and day out is different.

When push comes to shove, our differences, whether as individuals or as nations, are what make the world an interesting place. We can learn a lot from these differences just by being open to them, by looking at them as signs of an interconnected world. And we can use what we learn to become better, more understanding people. By respecting others for who they are, we respect ourselves for who we are. We may not always agree with someone else's opinion or way of life, but we can certainly learn to accept it. When that happens, we're ready for just about any conflict that comes our way.

<<< Bullies Made Easy >>>

4

Unfortunately, as you've probably figured out by now, not all people are friendly. Some people will never learn to respect individual differences. This fact throws a big, fat obstacle into the path of peaceful conflict resolution.

It's not hard to picture yourself working out a solution to a disagreement when that conflict is due to a difference in opinion or cultural background. It's easy to see why one person would like red, whereas another likes yellow. But when a conflict arises because someone is just plain mean—maybe he does-n't like you because you wear glasses, for

instance—resolving that conflict becomes much more difficult. He might pick on you. He might try to make you uncomfortable in front of your classmates. How to defend yourself, to stand up for yourself and your individuality, is not an easy question to answer.

Bullies. Every school has them, and so do many neighborhoods. Nobody likes them. They taunt, jeer, and try to start fights. They pick on kids and make fun of anyone who is not exactly like them. They're the bad apples. If you had a choice, you'd avoid them like the plague. Unfortunately, no matter what you do, they'll always be there somewhere. It's one of the realities of growing up—you've got to deal with those who don't.

When you're faced with a conflict thanks to one

In the lunch line at the school cafeteria one day, Jason suddenly finds himself in a world of trouble. Brutus, the school bully, well known for his tendency to torture small animals and eat other kids' homework assignments, decides that it's his turn for the mashed peas.

Brutus scoops up a handful of the green slime, turns to Jason, and slathers the food all over his backpack. Laughing hysterically, Brutus steps back, drops his tray on the floor, and puts his fists into the air. Hissing into Jason's face, he taunts, "Come on wimp, let's go!"

person's need to cause trouble, it's up to you to keep things in perspective and maintain the peace. Fighting a bully just gives him exactly what he wants and takes everything away from you. By falling for his tactics, you fail to respect yourself as an individual. You fail to see the main difference between you and him: the ability to tolerate.

Bullies are unable to tolerate differences between individuals. They pick on both the weak and the strong, anybody who stands out from the rest. They instigate—or try to start—arguments and fights. Why? It might be because of the way they were brought up or because they feel that they have no friends and need attention. Maybe they just don't fit in anywhere and can't think of any other way to express themselves. Whatever the reason, it doesn't justify their behavior, and it is not going to solve their problems.

The bottom line is that a bully is out to cause trouble, and the only way for you to bring an end to that trouble is by facing it like a man.

Facing it like a man does not mean that you have to fight. In fact, it means just the opposite. If a bully tries to instigate a physical conflict with you—by shoving, tripping, or verbally taunting you—you can easily win the battle by refusing to stoop to his level. Keep your wits together and use your brain, and you'll find that dealing with bullies is easy.

Knowing when to walk away from a conflict is extremely important. In general, turning your back on a

Jason, a star on the wrestling team, knows that he could take down Brutus with a few quick moves. But he also knows the consequences that a fight may bring—detention, suspension . . . he might even lose his spot on the team. Finally, he knows what Brutus wants: a brawl. He's not going to give it to him.

Jason calmly takes off his backpack and scrapes the mashed peas off the fabric and onto his plate. "Thanks for the peas, Brutus. They look delicious." Jason shoulders his pack and walks away to find a table where he can eat the rest of his lunch in peace. Brutus, left standing over his spilled tray in the middle of the lunch line, finds himself faced with a big mess instead of a fight.

conflict is not a good idea. It only serves to avoid the issue, to bury it so that it can be dug up again later. But when it comes to bullies—to people who want to start a fight just for the sake of fighting—it's time to turn the other cheek, so to speak. Sticking around will only give them what they want.

Get Creative!

Few people would deny that the mind is a powerful tool. Even fewer people have the courage to actually put their minds to work to find creative solutions to the world's toughest problems. That's exactly what Children's Creative Response to Conflict (CCRC) teaches people how to do. Established in 1972, CCRC tries to give young people and adults the skills they need to find nonviolent and creative solutions to conflict. The organization conducts thousands of workshops in schools and communities around the world. It teaches people about cooperation, communication, problem solving, and conflict resolution. If you think that the kids at your school could use a lesson or two on how to get creative, give CCRC a ring! For more information, contact CCRC at P.O. Box 271, 521 North Broadway, Nyack, New York 10960; (914) 353-1796. You can e-mail them at ccrcnyack@aol.com.

5

<<< Head Games >>>

If you're going to resolve conflicts peacefully, you have to learn to use your head. Those fists you've seen your hands curl into in the past? Forget about them. They're no good here. You can leave your knuckles to dangle by your sides. In the world of real resolution—where conflicts are put to rest for good—the only muscle you'll need is your brain.

Conflicts, especially ones that have the potential to explode, can be tricky. It's easy to jump to conclusions sometimes or assume that the other person means one thing when he actually means another. If the other person is angry, chances are he may not be thinking clearly and might not express himself well. Likewise, the same can happen to you. Emotions can be very strong and can change the way you see things. If you step back and look at the situation with a clear head, you may be able to bring the conflict down to size.

Just about any conflict can be resolved with a little creativity and a lot of patience. Next time you're faced with a difficult conflict, one that appears to be impossible to work out, think again. If you put your mind to work, you'll probably find an answer. Consider applying the following steps toward conflict resolution:

> Six Easy Steps to Conflict Resolution <

1 Stay cool. Take a step back and calm down. If it helps, take a deep breath. Think about what you're going to say before you say it. When you're ready to talk without blowing up, without fighting or interrupting, look the other person in the eye and ask if he's willing to do the same.

2 Talk it out. Express to the other person exactly how you feel. Don't argue. Just put your thoughts on the table as clearly as you can. Verbalize. When you've finished talking, ask the other person if he understands your point of view. Ask him to tell you what he thinks you said in his own words.

3 Listen. What does the other person have to say? Be considerate and listen to him very carefully. When he's finished, tell him in your own words what you think he said.

4 Define the problem. It's time to get to the heart of the matter. Express what you feel the problem is, then ask him to say what he thinks the problem is. See if you can both agree.

5 Think about it. Keep talking and try to work things out. How can you both bring an end to the problem? Can you make a truce that you're both happy with? Can you agree on the issue? If you disagree, can you at least disagree peacefully?

6 Wrap it up. By now, either you've come to a resolution, or things need to be taken to the next level. If the problem is solved, shake hands and thank the other person for working things out peacefully. If there are still important issues to be resolved, you may need to get help from a teacher, your parents, or someone else who is willing to listen to both sides of the story.

You can see that these steps don't leave a whole lot of room for fighting. Rather, the entire process depends on slowing down and giving both parties time to think. Nothing is rushed. Everything is slow, cool, and planned. You don't run away from the issue. Instead, you dive into it and tackle it headfirst. If you and the other person—the other disputant—can figure out a way to work on the problem together, it's only a matter of time before you'll reach a resolution.

Unfortunately, such thoughtful consideration of a problem doesn't always work. Take the case of the bully in the last chapter, for instance. All he wanted to do was start a fight. In cases like that, you may not be able to get the other person to calm down and talk. In that situation, it's best to stay cool on your side no matter what happens on the other side. If you can show the other person that fighting is not an option, he'll have nowhere to go with his fists. And if he persists—pushing you, calling you names, doing anything he can to get you to fight back—you can always get help. Sometimes the best solution to a conflict is finding an adult.

Peaceful People: Martin Luther King Jr.

Born: January 15, 1929, in Atlanta, Georgia

Died: Assassinated April 4, 1968, in Memphis, Tennessee

Great Quote: "Today the choice is no longer between violence and nonviolence. It is either non-violence or nonexistence."

When it comes to the battle for civil rights—the rights of every U.S. citizen to the individual freedom and dignity promised in the Declaration of Independence and the Constitution—Martin Luther King Jr. will forever be remembered as a hero. King, the winner of the 1964 Nobel Peace Prize, was the leader of the civil rights movement, a nationwide struggle for racial equality between blacks and whites. King brought black people and white people together and asked that they work—nonviolently—to fulfill his dream: the establishment of a nation where, at last, individuals would "not be judged by the color of their skin but by the content of their character."

Sadly, many others in the United States opposed this vision, and King and his followers were subjected to unrelenting harassment and vicious brutality. At many of their demonstrations, they were spat upon and beaten—sometimes by the police. Many of them were arrested, lost their jobs, had their homes bombed, and were even killed. Throughout it all, King never once turned his back on his belief in nonviolence. Instead, he brought about change through peaceful marches and electrifying speeches, teaching that the only way justice could be won was by people working together. Courage, he preached, was best displayed in peace, an ideal he carried with him all the way to his death at the hands of an assassin in Memphis, Tennessee, in April 1968.

6

<<< Negotiating for Peace >>>

You've probably heard the term "peace process" on the news. You know—presidents, prime ministers, diplomats, and other serious-looking officials crowded around an enormous oak table, working out the details of an agreement to end a war or other international conflict. They're talking, shaking hands, patting each other on the back, and hustling back and forth between issues in what seems to be an endless discussion about nothing at all. Those politicians may seem to be far removed from anything you've ever experienced, but in reality, you can learn a lot from them.

Negotiating is all about giving and receiving, finding a middle road so that both sides are happy. In a negotiation, neither side gets everything it wants; both sides have to sacrifice something. Those politicians may be deciding which territories should go to one party or the other, or how much money one group will have to give another in return for some important service. In your case, the terms are a little more down-to-earth.

You'd be surprised how often you negotiate without even realizing it. Every day you're faced with situations in which you have to negotiate. When you work out a deal with your parents to stay up late and watch your favorite television show in return for finishing your homework early, you're negotiating. When you get together with your friends for a game of pick-up basketball and choose teams, you're negotiating.

You're trying to make things fair, to level the playing field so that everyone is content. When two people negotiate, they talk about their interests and their needs and try to come up with a way to reach an agreement so that they can both be satisfied. Communication is very important—without it neither side has a chance to express itself. If you don't explain why you want to stay up late, for example, your parents won't have any reason to let you do so. If you don't allow everyone else to help pick teams, you'll probably end up with a lopsided basketball game. Make your thoughts clear, and you'll do just fine in the negotiating process.

Rob: "Scott should play on our team because we need a tall player. Besides, you already have Mark, who's not only tall but can dribble a basketball better than any of us can even walk."

John: "But Mark sprained his ankle last weekend, so he's only at half-speed. If you take Scott, you guys will destroy us!"

Eric: "I've got an idea. This game is just for fun. Let's put Scott on Rob's team for the first half, then switch him to John's team for the second half."

Scott: "That's fine with me, but what do I get if my team wins?"

Sometimes people or groups find it impossible to negotiate face-to-face. For one reason or another, they just can't communicate effectively. Whether it's because they're too embarrassed to look each other in the eye or too angry to remain calm during the negotiation process, there's just no way they can talk to one another. When that happens, one option is to use what is known as a mediator. A mediator is a neutral third party—someone who can look at both sides of a conflict without favoring either. The mediator's job is to help the disputing parties go over their options, express their thoughts, and reach an agreement. With well-directed questions and a little bit of prodding, the mediator can usually get the parties to talk out their problems. Typically the mediator will lay out a number of rules for the disputants to follow, then guide them toward a resolution.

Good, solid negotiations, whether they take place face-to-face or through a mediator, can stop conflict in its tracks. If you're negotiating and keep a clear head, there's no chance for a conflict to blow up and lead to violence. Violence can take place only when there are no negotiations, when one party or the other decides that finding a balance won't work. Approach every conflict, big or small, with an open mind, and you'll find that negotiating comes naturally. It's quite simple, really: Talk, listen, and be fair.

Peaceful People: Mohandas Karamchand Gandhi
Born: October 2, 1869, in Porbandar, India
Died: Assassinated January 30, 1948, in New
   Delhi, India
Great Quote: "An eye for an eye will make the
   whole world go blind."

At a time when violence seems to be common
everywhere, in homes and schools, in towns and
cities, between nations, the philosophy of peace to
which Mohandas K. Gandhi devoted his life in the
first half of the twentieth century might easily be
forgotten. As a leader of India's movement for independence from Britain, Gandhi used nonviolent
protest, which he called satyagraha ("soul force"),
to bring about political change. His followers called
him the Mahatma, which means "great soul." In
large part because of Gandhi's tactics, which includ-
ed peaceful demonstrations and hunger strikes,
India gained its independence from Britain in 1947.
Gandhi, a thin, frail, poor man, proved to the world
that the mind is far stronger than any amount of
muscle. Those who adopted Gandhi's methods of
nonviolent civil disobedience to bring about change
in their own societies include Martin Luther King Jr.
and Nelson Mandela, the South African leader who
for more than forty years, led the movement to end
South Africa's apartheid regime.

Become a Mediator

Many schools have mediation programs to help students resolve conflicts peacefully. In fact, according to the National Association for Mediation in Education (NAME), there are more than 5,000 schools in the United States with conflict management programs.Very often the mediators in these programs are other students. Student mediators are trained by teachers or other professionals and are taught how to maintain the peace among their classmates. If you think that you'd be a good mediator, ask a teacher or guidance counselor if your school has a program. If it doesn't, try to get one started.

<<< The Meaning of Manliness >>>

7

"So," you might ask, "what does all this nonviolent peace-and-love stuff have to do with the fact that I'm a guy?"

Well, nothing. Resolving conflict peacefully is important for anyone, whether they're a guy or a girl. The truth is, guys are much more likely than girls to use their fists or resort to violence to get what they want. For some reason—blame it on bad luck—many guys like to duke it out, to prove that they're stronger than other guys. But obviously that's a generalization, and there are plenty of examples of girls beating up on each other for many different reasons.

The purpose of this book is not to suggest that all guys are violent or that all guys need help learning how to resolve conflicts peacefully. Instead, it's to point out the fact that we live in a world full of conflict and that to deal with those conflicts successfully, we have to take on certain responsibilities—like learning how to cooperate, communicate, negotiate, and appreciate. As a guy, how you handle these responsibilities will eventually determine what kind of man you become. If you can commit yourself to resolving every conflict without the use of force, to using your brain instead of your brawn, you'll find that the road to a rewarding life is smooth and easy to travel. Figure out how to resolve conflicts, and you can find an answer to just about any problem you come across in life. If you can do that, realize find that being a guy isn't so tough after all.

>> Get to Work! <<

If you become really good at resolving conflicts, you may decide that you want to make a career of it. Schools, court systems, community organizations . . . you name it, just about everywhere you look there's a need for people who can maintain the peace. Here's a partial list of the many interesting jobs out there in the working world that require people who are trained in the field of conflict management.

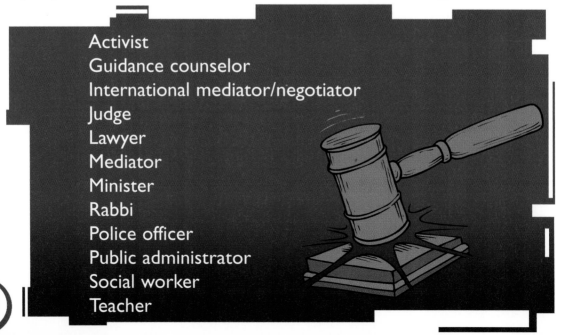

Activist
Guidance counselor
International mediator/negotiator
Judge
Lawyer
Mediator
Minister
Rabbi
Police officer
Public administrator
Social worker
Teacher

>> What Does Nonviolence Mean, Anyway? <<

In the dictionary, "nonviolence" is defined as "abstention from violence as a matter of principle." Big words, yes, but not quite a big enough definition. Nonviolence means more than avoiding violence. It also means acting in ways that bring an end to violence. What follows is a list of things you can do to win the peaceful battle against violence.

Forgive yourself and others for mistakes.

Teach others how to live in peace.

Try to be fair and kind in everything you do.

Treat everyone and everything with respect.

Tackle your problems peacefully.

Be considerate of others' opinions and beliefs.

Celebrate differences and treat them as opportunities to learn and grow.

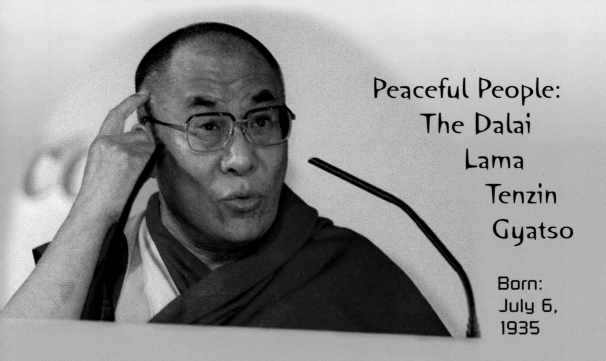

Peaceful People: The Dalai Lama Tenzin Gyatso

Born: July 6, 1935

Great Quote: "I believe all suffering is caused by ignorance. People inflict pain on others in the selfish pursuit of their happiness or satisfaction. Yet true happiness comes from a sense of brotherhood and sisterhood. We need to cultivate a universal responsibility for each other and the planet we share."

Although he always describes himself as "just a simple Buddhist monk, nothing more, nothing less," the Dalai Lama is perhaps the most well-known advocate of nonviolence in the world today. The winner of the 1989 Nobel Peace Prize, the Dalai Lama is the spiritual leader of the people of Tibet and the head of state of the Tibetan government in exile.

The Dalai Lama was born Lhamo Dhondrub on July 6, 1935, in Taktser, a small agricultural village in northwestern Tibet. At the age of two, he was recognized as the fourteenth reincarnation of the Dalai Lama. According to Tibetan tradition, the Dalai Lama is the living incarnation of Avalokitesvara, the Buddha of Compassion, and is the spiritual and political leader of the nation of Tibet.

Tibet is a nation at the center of Asia that is roughly the size of western Europe and is ringed by the highest mountains in the world. It was overrun and occupied by troops from the People's Republic of China in 1950, the same year that the Dalai Lama took full political power. When an uprising by the Tibetan people nine years later was brutally repressed by the Chinese, the Dalai Lama and 80,000 Tibetan refugees went into exile. Since that time, from his government's headquarters in Dharamsala, India, the Dalai Lama has worked tirelessly to focus the world's attention on finding a peaceful solution for the situation in his homeland.

The Dalai Lama's proposal is that all of Tibet be transformed into what he calls a zone of Ahimsa, or peace sanctuary. Specifically, that would mean that all of Tibet would be demilitarized, with the manufacture, use, or testing of any types of weaponry prohibited. The Tibetan plateau would be transformed into the world's largest natural park. Tibet would become a sanctuary for world organizations devoted to human rights and the preservation of the environment.

Although these proposals for Tibet have not yet become a reality, the Dalai Lama has become an inspirational leader for peoples around the globe, not just Tibetans and Buddhists. As the Nobel Prize committee put it, "The Dalai Lama has developed his philosophy from a great reverence for all things living and upon the concept of universal responsibility."

aggression   An attack or other forceful action against someone or something.

conflict   An argument or dispute between two or more parties with different interests, needs, wishes, or perspectives that they believe to be incompatible.

cooperate   To act or work together.

dialogue   A discussion between conflicting parties that is meant to bring about a resolution.

disputant   A person involved in a dispute.

dispute   An argument or disagreement.

empathize   To understand the thoughts and feelings of another person.

intergroup conflict   A conflict between groups or organizations.

international conflict   A conflict between nations.

interpersonal conflict   A conflict between two or more individuals.

intrapersonal conflict   A conflict within an individual.

mediate   To work as the middleperson between conflicting parties in order to bring about a resolution.

mediation   An intervention between conflicting parties in order to bring about a resolution.

mediator   A peacemaker or negotiator.

negotiate   To settle or bring about by mutual agreement.

negotiator   One who tries to settle a conflict by bringing the conflicting parties to an agreement.

opinion   Belief or view.

peer   An equal in standing.

perspective/position   Point of view.

prejudice   A judgment or opinion formed without a thorough
understanding of all the facts.

reconciliation   An agreement.

resolution   A conclusion or settlement.

solution   An answer or result to a problem.

tolerance   The ability to understand and accept beliefs, prac-
tices, or opinions that are different from your own.

<<< It's a Guy's World >>>

HELPFUL ORGANIZATIONS

Children's Creative Response to Conflict Program
521 North Broadway, Box 271
Nyack, NY 10960
(914) 353-1796
e-mail: ccrcnyack@aol.com

Conflict Resolution Education Network
1527 New Hampshire Avenue NW
Washington, DC 20036
(202) 667-9700
Web site: http://www.CREnet.org

CRU Institute
845 106th Avenue NE, Suite 109
Bellevue, WA 98004
(800) 922-1988 or (206) 451-4015
Web site: http://www.conflictnet.org/cru/

Educators for Social Responsibility
23 Garden Street
Cambridge, MA 02138
(617) 492-1764
Web site: http://www.esrnational.org.

The Ohio Commission on Dispute Resolution and Conflict Management
77 South High Street, 24th Floor
Columbus, OH 43266-0124
(614) 752-9595
Web site: http://www.state.oh.us/cdr/

Peace Education Foundation
1900 Biscayne Boulevard
Miami, FL 33132-1025
(800) 749-8838 or (305) 576-5075
Web site: http://www.peace-ed.org.

Resolving Conflict Creatively Program (a program of Educators for Social Responsibility)
40 Exchange Place, Suite 1111
New York, NY 10005
(212) 509-0022
Web site: http://www.esrnational.org

HELPFUL WEB SITES

Adolescence Directory On-Line
www.education.indiana.edu/cas/adol/adol.html

Conflict Resolution Resource Center
www.conflict-resolution.net

Mediation Information and Resource Center
www.mediate.com

Nonviolence Network
www.nonviolence.net

<<< Get Booked >>>

BOOKS

Kreiner, Anna. *Everything You Need to Know About School Violence.* New York: Rosen Publishing Group, 1996.

Nathan, Amy. *Everything You Need to Know About Conflict Resolution.* New York: Rosen Publishing Group, 1996.

Rue, Nancy. *Everything You Need to Know About Peer Mediation.* New York: Rosen Publishing Group, 1997.

Ury, William. *Getting Past No: Negotiating with Difficult People.* New York: Bantam Books, 1991.

Weeks, Dudley. *The Eight Essential Steps to Conflict Resolution.* New York: G.P. Putnam's Sons, 1992.

<<< Index >>>

<<< Credits >>>

About the Author
Chris Hayhurst is a freelance journalist living in northern Colorado.

Photo Credits

Series Design and Layout
Oliver H. Rosenberg